WELCOME TO

YOUR CRUISE

ABOARD THE

DESTINATION

EMBARKATION DATE

THIS JOURNAL BELONGS TO

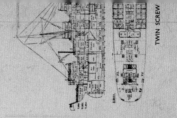
TWIN SCREW

Go forth seeking adventure. Open your eyes, your ears, your mind, your heart, your spirit and you'll find adventure everywhere.

HOW TO USE THIS JOURNAL

Besides the bounty of seafaring advice and traveling tips, this user-friendly journal provides beautiful pages to record all your experiences, whether calm and relaxing or over-the-top adventurous. We've divided the journaling area into easy-to-use segments to help you document a cruise up to a month long.

The journaling section is set up in four-page segments. If you use one segment (four pages) a day you will cover a twenty-eight day cruise. Using four segments (sixteen pages) per day allows you to be very detailed each day for a seven day cruise. Add in notes and lists, tape in ticket stubs and photos, or fill it with doodles or sketches. The journey is yours; fill the pages with your holiday adventure.

4

TABLE OF CONTENTS

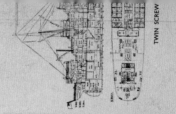

TWIN SCREW

PLANNING TIPS

Getting there is half the fun of your cruising holiday. For your convenience we've included a few pages of the very important pre-departure planning tips.

THINGS TO DO BEFORE YOU LEAVE:

_____ Ask neighbor to watch house/water plants
_____ Call credit card companies*
_____ Get cash from the bank
_____ Give emergency numbers to family members
_____ Give itinerary to family members
_____ Lock all windows/doors
_____ Put lights and radio on a timer
_____ Stop mail/newspapers
_____ Take pet(s) to kennel/sitter

*A courtesy call to your credit card company to inform them of your trip will help assure them of your whereabouts and they won't suspect fraud and subsequently place a hold on your card for suspicious charges. Let them know when you will be going out of the country and places you will be visiting.

**THE TOP TEN LIST OF SOURCE COUNTRIES WHERE
PASSENGERS EMBARK ON A CRUISE SHIP:**

10. Scandinavia & Finland

9. France

8. Spain

7. Canada

6. Brazil

5. Australia & New Zealand

4. Italy

3. Germany

2. UK & Ireland

AND THE NUMBER ONE COUNTRY TO EMBARK ON A CRUISE:

The United States of America

WHAT IS THE NUMBER ONE CRUISE TREND?

Improved Internet connectivity at sea.

THE HOTTEST NEW CRUISE DESTINATION THIS YEAR?

Trans Pacific

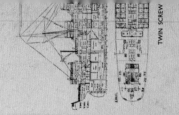

NATURAL SEA SICKNESS/MOTION SICKNESS REMEDIES

Sea sickness is generally caused by a sensory overload when your eyes send visual signals to your brain that don't seem to match the sensation your inner ear is experiencing and sending to your brain. The result is often an upset stomach, sweating, light-headedness, or hyperventilation. (Please visit the onboard physician if symptoms persist or are severe.)

Don't feel bad if you're affected by these symptoms as even NASA astronauts and military fighter pilots often struggle with these same issues.

One of the best natural ways to combat motion or sea sickness is somewhat counter intuitive: Do not lie down and rest in your cabin. Experiencing the ship's motion will make you feel worse.

Ginger is your best natural herbal remedy. Any of the stewards onboard will be able to provide you with a small teaspoon size amount. Dice it into small bits and swallow it whole, ideally with a splash of ginger ale.

Then make your way to a rail and look out to the furthest point on the horizon. Your eyes will see that the ship is almost completely stable and still. Breathe deeply the fresh sea air and think about all the fun you'll soon be enjoying on the cruise.

PACKING TIPS

Every cruise line has their own suggestions and recommendations for the dinner hour and evening wear, however day wear is very casual. That said, your first day of embarkation will typically not allow you easy access to your luggage until it arrives in your stateroom, often hours after sailing. So be sure to bring a carry-on bag that includes bathing suits, sunscreen, deck shoes, medications, some light toiletries, and perhaps a change of clothes or beach cover up. If you're traveling with young children be sure to pack enough diapers and wipes for several hours.

If you'll be traveling with Smartphones or laptops (resist the temptation—you're on vacation), be sure to pack your phone chargers and a compact voltage conversion set, although most cruise ships have various voltage outlets.

Don't bother with hair dryers, they'll be provided in your stateroom. Besides this is the time to truly let the wind blow in your hair.

Some well-traveled cruisers suggest a few clothespins to keep curtains closed and the early morning sunshine out until you're ready to face the day. A night-light is another suggestion if you prefer it or if you're traveling with small children.

Extra-large Ziplock bags have dozens of uses from storing wet bathing suits to storing sunscreen, medications, or snacks for the little ones.

Resist the temptation to overpack. The onboard gift shops carry most everything you'll need that you may have forgotten to bring. The extra space and weight you'll save is well worth the money spent onboard.

Look to see if your cruise line allows you to pre-book services online such as trips to the spa and shoreside excursions. It's a great way to beat the rush and reserve the best dates and times.

If you've booked your passage with a cruise travel agent, be sure to ask their advice on "dos and don'ts." They are experts in cruise line travel and can provide you wonderful advice to make your sailing trip a memorable one.

SUGGESTED SUPPLIES

When preparing to travel, lay out all your clothes and all your money.
Then take half the clothes and twice the money.
SUSAN HELLER

CLOTHES

_____ Dress clothes for formal dining/parties
_____ Dress and casual shoes
_____ Exercise clothes/shoes
_____ Hats/Visor
_____ Pajamas
_____ Resort casual wear
_____ Swimsuits
_____ Swimsuit cover-up

DOCUMENTS

_____ Airline tickets
_____ Credit cards (2)
_____ Cruise line contact information
_____ Cruise line **Boarding Passes** and materials
_____ Emergency contact information
_____ Hotel confirmations
_____ Medical insurance cards
_____ Luggage tags
_____ Passport (and one copy) and birth certificate
_____ Photo ID/driver's license (and one copy)
_____ Proof of auto insurance or International Drivers License

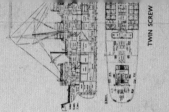
TWIN SCREW

MEDICINES

_____ Anti-bacterial ointment
_____ Anti-diarrhea/Anti-acid
_____ Hand sanitizer
_____ Motion sickness pills
_____ Pain reliever
_____ **Prescriptions**

MY MEDICATIONS:

Medication #1: _____
Medication #2: _____
Medication #3: _____
Allergies: _____

Blood Type: _____   Rh: _____
Primary doctor's contact info: _____
_____
_____

MY SPOUSE'S MEDICATIONS:

Medication #1: _____
Medication #2: _____
Medication #3: _____
Allergies: _____

Blood Type: _____   Rh: _____
Primary doctor's contact info: _____
_____
_____

TOILETRIES

____ Comb/brush	____ Mouthwash
____ Contact lens solution	____ Nail polish
____ Curling iron	____ Perfume/cologne
____ Deodorant	____ Shaving items
____ Floss	____ Toothbrush and paste
____ Makeup/remover	

MISCELLANEOUS ITEMS

____ Binoculars

____ Books/audio books

____ Bungee cord & clothes pins

____ Camera (extra memory cards or film)

____ CASH

____ Cell phone and charger

____ Daypack/waistpack

____ Duct tape (repair damaged bags or hems)

____ Extra batteries

____ Extra glasses/contact lenses

____ Extra set of car keys

____ Jewelry

____ Lint brush

____ Night-light

____ Cruise Journal, pen, highlighter

____ Sunglasses

____ Sunscreen/burn lotion

____ Travel clock/alarm clock (Smartphones have an app)

____ Ziplock bags (large and small)

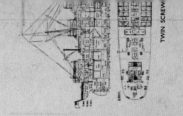

DATE: _____

LOCATION/PORT OF CALL: _____

_____

WEATHER: _____

ACTIVITIES: _____

_____

_____

_____

_____

_____

_____

_____

_____

_____

MEALS & DINING: _____

_____

_____

_____

_____

_____

_____

_____

_____

DATE: _____

_____

_____

_____

_____

_____

_____

_____

_____

_____

_____

_____

_____

_____

_____

_____

_____

_____

_____

It is God to whom and with whom we travel, and while He is the end of our journey,
He is also at every stopping place.

ELISABETH ELLIOT

DATE: _____

_____

_____

_____

_____

_____

_____

_____

_____

_____

_____

_____

_____

_____

_____

_____

_____

_____

_____

_____

_____

DATE: _____

_____

_____

_____

_____

_____

_____

_____

_____

_____

_____

_____

_____

_____

_____

_____

_____

_____

_____

_____

We cannot discover new oceans until we have the courage to lose sight of the shore.

MURIEL CHEN

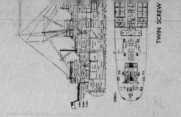

TWIN SCREW

DATE: _____

LOCATION/PORT OF CALL: _____

_____

WEATHER: _____

ACTIVITIES: _____

_____

_____

_____

_____

_____

_____

_____

_____

MEALS & DINING: _____

_____

_____

_____

_____

_____

_____

_____

DATE: _____

_____

_____

_____

_____

_____

_____

_____

_____

_____

_____

_____

_____

_____

_____

_____

_____

_____

_____

Every day is an opportunity to make a new happy ending.
May you live all the days of your life.
JONATHAN SWIFT

DATE: _____

_____

_____

_____

_____

_____

_____

_____

_____

_____

_____

_____

_____

_____

_____

_____

_____

_____

_____

_____

_____

DATE: _____

_____

_____

_____

_____

_____

_____

_____

_____

_____

_____

_____

_____

_____

_____

_____

_____

_____

_____

_____

_____

Life [is] a glorious experience of discovering God's endless wonders.
WENDY MOORE

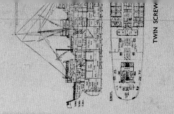

DATE: _____

LOCATION/PORT OF CALL: _____

_____

WEATHER: _____

ACTIVITIES: _____

_____

_____

_____

_____

_____

_____

_____

_____

MEALS & DINING: _____

_____

_____

_____

_____

_____

_____

_____

DATE: _____

_____

_____

_____

_____

_____

_____

_____

_____

_____

_____

_____

_____

_____

_____

_____

_____

_____

I travel not to go anywhere, but to go. I travel for travel's sake.
The great affair is to move.

ROBERT LOUIS STEVENSON

DATE: _____

_____

_____

_____

_____

_____

_____

_____

_____

_____

_____

_____

_____

_____

_____

_____

_____

_____

_____

_____

_____

DATE: _____

_____

_____

_____

_____

_____

_____

_____

_____

_____

_____

_____

_____

_____

_____

_____

_____

_____

_____

_____

I am with you and will watch over you wherever you go.

GENESIS 28:15 NIV

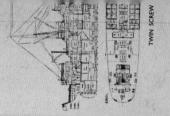

TWIN SCREW

DATE: _____

LOCATION/PORT OF CALL: _____

_____

WEATHER: _____

ACTIVITIES: _____

_____

_____

_____

_____

_____

_____

_____

MEALS & DINING: _____

_____

_____

_____

_____

_____

_____

DATE: _____

_____

_____

_____

_____

_____

_____

_____

_____

_____

_____

_____

_____

_____

_____

_____

_____

_____

_____

_____

Take a chance! All life is a chance. The one who goes furthest is generally the one who is willing to do and dare.

DALE CARNEGIE

DATE: _____

_____

_____

_____

_____

_____

_____

_____

_____

_____

_____

_____

_____

_____

_____

_____

_____

_____

_____

_____

_____

_____

DATE: _____

_____

_____

_____

_____

_____

_____

_____

_____

_____

_____

_____

_____

_____

_____

_____

_____

_____

I dare say I am compelled, unconsciously compelled, now to write volume after volume, as in past years I was compelled to go to sea, voyage after voyage.

JOSEPH CONRAD

TWIN SCREW

DATE: _____

LOCATION/PORT OF CALL: _____

_____

WEATHER: _____

ACTIVITIES: _____

_____

_____

_____

_____

_____

_____

_____

_____

_____

MEALS & DINING: _____

_____

_____

_____

_____

_____

_____

_____

_____

DATE: _____

_____

_____

_____

_____

_____

_____

_____

_____

_____

_____

_____

_____

_____

_____

_____

_____

_____

_____

_____

_____

_____

_____

*Life…gives you the chance to love and to work and to play
and to look up at the stars.*

HENRY VAN DYKE

DATE: _____

_____

_____

_____

_____

_____

_____

_____

_____

_____

_____

_____

_____

_____

_____

_____

_____

_____

_____

_____

DATE: _____

_____

_____

_____

_____

_____

_____

_____

_____

_____

_____

_____

_____

_____

_____

_____

_____

_____

_____

_____

_____

I think you travel to search and you come back home to find yourself there.
CHIMAMANDA NGOZI ADICHIE

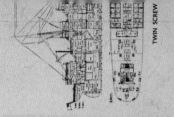

TWIN SCREW

DATE: _____

LOCATION/PORT OF CALL: _____

_____

WEATHER: _____

ACTIVITIES: _____

_____

_____

_____

_____

_____

_____

_____

_____

MEALS & DINING: _____

_____

_____

_____

_____

_____

_____

_____

DATE: _____

_____

_____

_____

_____

_____

_____

_____

_____

_____

_____

_____

_____

_____

_____

_____

_____

_____

*Think of whatever you are doing as an adventure
and watch your life change for the better.*

WILFERD A. PETERSON

DATE: _____

_____

_____

_____

_____

_____

_____

_____

_____

_____

_____

_____

_____

_____

_____

_____

_____

_____

_____

_____

_____

DATE: _____

_____

_____

_____

_____

_____

_____

_____

_____

_____

_____

_____

_____

_____

_____

_____

_____

_____

_____

_____

_____

Life begins each morning.... Each morning is the open door to a new world—
new vistas, new aims, new tryings.
LEIGH MITCHELL HODGES

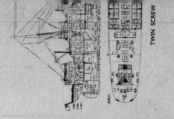

TWIN SCREW

DATE: _____

LOCATION/PORT OF CALL: _____

_____

WEATHER: _____

ACTIVITIES: _____

_____

_____

_____

_____

_____

_____

_____

_____

MEALS & DINING: _____

_____

_____

_____

_____

_____

_____

DATE: _____

_____

_____

_____

_____

_____

_____

_____

_____

_____

_____

_____

_____

_____

_____

_____

_____

_____

_____

_____

Travel far enough, you meet yourself.
DAVID MITCHELL

DATE: _____

_____

_____

_____

_____

_____

_____

_____

_____

_____

_____

_____

_____

_____

_____

_____

_____

_____

_____

_____

_____

DATE: _____

_____

_____

_____

_____

_____

_____

_____

_____

_____

_____

_____

_____

_____

_____

_____

_____

_____

_____

*We need the tonic of wildness.... At the same time that we are earnest to explore
and learn all things, we require that all things be mysterious and unexplorable,
that land and sea be indefinitely wild, unsurveyed and unfathomed.*

HENRY DAVID THOREAU

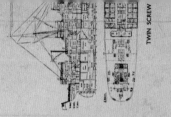

TWIN SCREW

DATE: _____

LOCATION/PORT OF CALL: _____

_____

WEATHER: _____

ACTIVITIES: _____

_____

_____

_____

_____

_____

_____

_____

_____

MEALS & DINING: _____

_____

_____

_____

_____

_____

_____

_____

DATE: _____

_____

_____

_____

_____

_____

_____

_____

_____

_____

_____

_____

_____

_____

_____

_____

_____

_____

_____

_____

Like all great travelers, I have seen more than I remember,
and remember more than I have seen.

BENJAMIN DISRAELI

DATE: _____

_____

_____

_____

_____

_____

_____

_____

_____

_____

_____

_____

_____

_____

_____

_____

_____

_____

_____

_____

_____

DATE: _____

_____

_____

_____

_____

_____

_____

_____

_____

_____

_____

_____

_____

_____

_____

_____

_____

_____

_____

_____

_____

When I look back at where I've been, I see that what I am becoming
is a whole lot further down the road from where I was.

GLORIA GAITHER

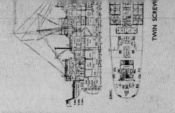

DATE: _____

LOCATION/PORT OF CALL: _____
_____

WEATHER: _____

ACTIVITIES: _____
_____
_____
_____
_____
_____
_____
_____
_____

MEALS & DINING: _____
_____
_____
_____
_____
_____
_____
_____

DATE: _____

_____

_____

_____

_____

_____

_____

_____

_____

_____

_____

_____

_____

_____

_____

_____

_____

_____

_____

You see me when I travel and when I rest at home. You know everything I do.

PSALM 139:3 NLT

DATE: _____

_____

_____

_____

_____

_____

_____

_____

_____

_____

_____

_____

_____

_____

_____

_____

_____

_____

_____

_____

_____

_____

DATE: _____

_____

_____

_____

_____

_____

_____

_____

_____

_____

_____

_____

_____

_____

_____

_____

_____

_____

_____

One way to get the most out of life is to look upon it as an adventure.
WILLIAM FEATHER

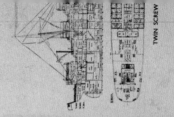

TWIN SCREW

DATE: _____

LOCATION/PORT OF CALL: _____

_____

WEATHER: _____

ACTIVITIES: _____

_____

_____

_____

_____

_____

_____

_____

MEALS & DINING: _____

_____

_____

_____

_____

_____

_____

_____

DATE: _____

_____

_____

_____

_____

_____

_____

_____

_____

_____

_____

_____

_____

_____

_____

_____

_____

_____

_____

_____

Wherever you go becomes a part of you somehow.
ANITA DESAI

DATE: _____

_____

_____

_____

_____

_____

_____

_____

_____

_____

_____

_____

_____

_____

_____

_____

_____

_____

_____

_____

_____

DATE: _____

_____

_____

_____

_____

_____

_____

_____

_____

_____

_____

_____

_____

_____

_____

_____

_____

_____

Look at that sea...all silver and shadow and vision of things not seen. We couldn't enjoy its loveliness any more if we had millions of dollars and ropes of diamonds.

L. M. MONTGOMERY

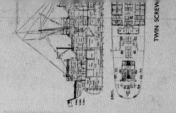

TWIN SCREW

DATE: _____

LOCATION/PORT OF CALL: _____

_____

WEATHER: _____

ACTIVITIES: _____

_____

_____

_____

_____

_____

_____

_____

_____

MEALS & DINING: _____

_____

_____

_____

_____

_____

_____

_____

DATE: _____

_____

_____

_____

_____

_____

_____

_____

_____

_____

_____

_____

_____

_____

_____

_____

_____

_____

_____

They travel lightly whom God's grace carries.

THOMAS A. KEMPIS

DATE: _____

_____

_____

_____

_____

_____

_____

_____

_____

_____

_____

_____

_____

_____

_____

_____

_____

_____

_____

_____

DATE: _____

_____

_____

_____

_____

_____

_____

_____

_____

_____

_____

_____

_____

_____

_____

_____

_____

_____

There is a tide in the affairs of men, which taken at the flood,
leads on to fortune. Omitted, all the voyage of their life is bound in shallows
and in miseries. On such a full sea are we now afloat. And we must
take the current when it serves, or lose our ventures.

WILLIAM SHAKESPEARE

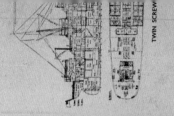

DATE: _____

LOCATION/PORT OF CALL: _____

_____

WEATHER: _____

ACTIVITIES: _____

_____

_____

_____

_____

_____

_____

_____

MEALS & DINING: _____

_____

_____

_____

_____

_____

_____

_____

DATE: _____

_____

_____

_____

_____

_____

_____

_____

_____

_____

_____

_____

_____

_____

_____

_____

_____

_____

_____

_____

Certainly, travel is more than the seeing of sights; it is a change that goes on, deep and permanent, in the ideas of living.

MIRIAM BEARD

DATE: _____

_____

_____

_____

_____

_____

_____

_____

_____

_____

_____

_____

_____

_____

_____

_____

_____

_____

_____

_____

_____

_____

DATE: _____

_____

_____

_____

_____

_____

_____

_____

_____

_____

_____

_____

_____

_____

_____

_____

_____

_____

_____

The larger the island of knowledge, the longer the shoreline of wonder.
RALPH W. SOCKMAN

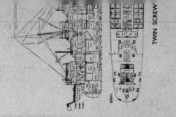

TWIN SCREW

DATE: _____

LOCATION/PORT OF CALL: _____

_____

WEATHER: _____

ACTIVITIES: _____

_____

_____

_____

_____

_____

_____

_____

_____

MEALS & DINING: _____

_____

_____

_____

_____

_____

_____

_____

DATE: _____

_____

_____

_____

_____

_____

_____

_____

_____

_____

_____

_____

_____

_____

_____

_____

_____

_____

May the road rise to meet you, may the wind be always at your back...
And, until we meet again, may God hold you in the palm of His hand.

IRISH BLESSING

DATE: _____

_____

_____

_____

_____

_____

_____

_____

_____

_____

_____

_____

_____

_____

_____

_____

_____

_____

_____

_____

_____

_____

_____

DATE: _____

_____

_____

_____

_____

_____

_____

_____

_____

_____

_____

_____

_____

_____

_____

_____

_____

_____

_____

_____

_____

_____

Your life is a journey you must travel with a deep consciousness of God.

1 PETER 1:18 MSG

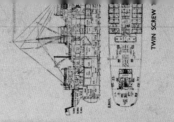

TWIN SCREW

DATE: _____

LOCATION/PORT OF CALL: _____
_____

WEATHER: _____

ACTIVITIES: _____
_____
_____
_____
_____
_____
_____
_____
_____
_____

MEALS & DINING: _____
_____
_____
_____
_____
_____
_____
_____
_____

DATE: _____

_____

_____

_____

_____

_____

_____

_____

_____

_____

_____

_____

_____

_____

_____

_____

_____

_____

_____

Life is not a journey to the grave with the intention of arriving safely in one pretty and well preserved piece, but to skid across the line broadside, thoroughly used up, worn out, leaking oil, shouting Geronimo!

BILL McKENNA

DATE: _____

_____

_____

_____

_____

_____

_____

_____

_____

_____

_____

_____

_____

_____

_____

_____

_____

_____

_____

_____

_____

_____

DATE: _____

_____

_____

_____

_____

_____

_____

_____

_____

_____

_____

_____

_____

_____

_____

_____

_____

_____

_____

_____

_____

Not all those who wander are lost.

J.R.R. TOLKIEN

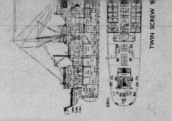

TWIN SCREW

DATE: _____

LOCATION/PORT OF CALL: _____

_____

WEATHER: _____

ACTIVITIES: _____

_____

_____

_____

_____

_____

_____

_____

_____

MEALS & DINING: _____

_____

_____

_____

_____

_____

_____

_____

_____

DATE: _____

_____

_____

_____

_____

_____

_____

_____

_____

_____

_____

_____

_____

_____

_____

_____

_____

_____

_____

_____

_____

_____

We are all travellers in the wilderness of this world, and the best that we find in our
travels is an honest friend. He is a fortunate voyager who finds many.

ROBERT LOUIS STEVENSON

DATE: _____

_____

_____

_____

_____

_____

_____

_____

_____

_____

_____

_____

_____

_____

_____

_____

_____

_____

_____

_____

_____

DATE: _____

_____

_____

_____

_____

_____

_____

_____

_____

_____

_____

_____

_____

_____

_____

_____

_____

_____

_____

_____

_____

_____

_____

Most new discoveries are suddenly-seen things that were always there.

SUSANNE K. LANGER

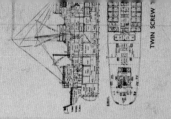
TWIN SCREW

DATE: _____

LOCATION/PORT OF CALL: _____

_____

WEATHER: _____

ACTIVITIES: _____

_____

_____

_____

_____

_____

_____

_____

_____

MEALS & DINING: _____

_____

_____

_____

_____

_____

_____

_____

_____

DATE: _____

_____

_____

_____

_____

_____

_____

_____

_____

_____

_____

_____

_____

_____

_____

_____

_____

_____

_____

_____

_____

For God's love is literally infinite. It is the shoreless sea we are destined to swim in, surf in, and grow in forever.

PETER KREEFT

DATE: _____

DATE: _____

_____

_____

_____

_____

_____

_____

_____

_____

_____

_____

_____

_____

_____

_____

_____

_____

To move, to breathe, to fly, to float,
To gain all while you give,
To roam the roads of lands remote,
To travel is to live.

HANS CHRISTIAN ANDERSEN

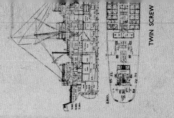

TWIN SCREW

DATE: _____

LOCATION/PORT OF CALL: _____

_____

WEATHER: _____

ACTIVITIES: _____

_____

_____

_____

_____

_____

_____

_____

_____

MEALS & DINING: _____

_____

_____

_____

_____

_____

_____

_____

DATE: _____

_____

_____

_____

_____

_____

_____

_____

_____

_____

_____

_____

_____

_____

_____

_____

_____

_____

There's not a place on earth's vast round,
In ocean's deep or air,
Where love and beauty are not found,
For God is everywhere.

DATE: _____

_____

_____

_____

_____

_____

_____

_____

_____

_____

_____

_____

_____

_____

_____

_____

_____

_____

_____

_____

DATE: _____

_____

_____

_____

_____

_____

_____

_____

_____

_____

_____

_____

_____

_____

_____

_____

_____

_____

_____

_____

_____

_____

_____

_____

Meeting someone for the first time is like going on a treasure hunt.
What wonderful worlds we can find in others!

EDWARD E. FORD

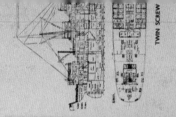

TWIN SCREW

DATE: _____

LOCATION/PORT OF CALL: _____

_____

WEATHER: _____

ACTIVITIES: _____

_____

_____

_____

_____

_____

_____

_____

_____

MEALS & DINING: _____

_____

_____

_____

_____

_____

_____

_____

_____

24 OCT 2013

DATE: _____

_____

_____

_____

_____

_____

_____

_____

_____

_____

_____

_____

_____

_____

_____

_____

_____

_____

_____

Once you have traveled, the voyage never ends, but is played out over and over again in the quietest chambers. The mind can never break off from the journey.

PAT CONROY

DATE: _____

_____

_____

_____

_____

_____

_____

_____

_____

_____

_____

_____

_____

_____

_____

_____

_____

_____

_____

_____

_____

_____

DATE: _____

_____

_____

_____

_____

_____

_____

_____

_____

_____

_____

_____

_____

_____

_____

_____

_____

_____

The longer I live, the more my mind dwells upon
the beauty and the wonder of the world.

JOHN BURROUGHS

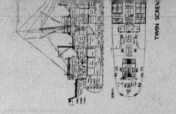

DATE: _____

LOCATION/PORT OF CALL: _____

_____

WEATHER: _____

ACTIVITIES: _____

_____

_____

_____

_____

_____

_____

_____

MEALS & DINING: _____

_____

_____

_____

_____

_____

_____

_____

DATE: _____

_____

_____

_____

_____

_____

_____

_____

_____

_____

_____

_____

_____

_____

_____

_____

_____

_____

_____

_____

Put your hope in the LORD. Travel steadily along his path.

PSALM 37:34 NLT

DATE: _____

_____

_____

_____

_____

_____

_____

_____

_____

_____

_____

_____

_____

_____

_____

_____

_____

_____

_____

_____

DATE: _____

_____

_____

_____

_____

_____

_____

_____

_____

_____

_____

_____

_____

_____

_____

_____

_____

_____

Anything, everything, little or big becomes an adventure
when the right person shares it.

KATHLEEN NORRIS

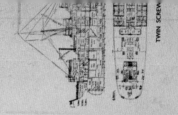
TWIN SCREW

DATE: _____

LOCATION/PORT OF CALL: _____

_____

WEATHER: _____

ACTIVITIES: _____

_____

_____

_____

_____

_____

_____

_____

_____

MEALS & DINING: _____

_____

_____

_____

_____

_____

_____

_____

DATE: _____

_____

_____

_____

_____

_____

_____

_____

_____

_____

_____

_____

_____

_____

_____

_____

_____

_____

_____

_____

_____

No journey carries one far unless, as it extends into the world around us,
it goes an equal distance into the world within.

LILLIAN SMITH

DATE: _____

_____

_____

_____

_____

_____

_____

_____

_____

_____

_____

_____

_____

_____

_____

_____

_____

_____

_____

_____

DATE: _____

_____

_____

_____

_____

_____

_____

_____

_____

_____

_____

_____

_____

_____

_____

_____

_____

The use of traveling is to regulate imagination by reality,
and instead of thinking how things may be, to see them as they are.

SAMUEL JOHNSON

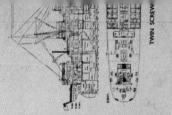
TWIN SCREW

DATE: _____

LOCATION/PORT OF CALL: _____
_____

WEATHER: _____

ACTIVITIES: _____
_____
_____
_____
_____
_____
_____
_____
_____

MEALS & DINING: _____
_____
_____
_____
_____
_____
_____
_____

DATE: _____

_____

_____

_____

_____

_____

_____

_____

_____

_____

_____

_____

_____

_____

_____

_____

_____

_____

_____

_____

_____

The treasure our heart searches for is found in the ocean of God's love.
JANET L. SMITH

DATE: _____

_____

_____

_____

_____

_____

_____

_____

_____

_____

_____

_____

_____

_____

_____

_____

_____

_____

_____

_____

_____

DATE: _____

_____

_____

_____

_____

_____

_____

_____

_____

_____

_____

_____

_____

_____

_____

_____

_____

_____

Isn't it splendid to think of all the things there are to find out about?
It just makes me feel glad to be alive—it's such an interesting world.

LUCY MAUD MONTGOMERY

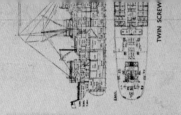

DATE: _____

LOCATION/PORT OF CALL: _____

_____

WEATHER: _____

ACTIVITIES: _____

_____

_____

_____

_____

_____

_____

_____

_____

MEALS & DINING: _____

_____

_____

_____

_____

_____

_____

_____

DATE: _____

_____

_____

_____

_____

_____

_____

_____

_____

_____

_____

_____

_____

_____

_____

_____

_____

_____

Though we travel the world over to find the beautiful,
we must carry it with us or we find it not.

RALPH WALDO EMERSON

DATE: _____

_____

_____

_____

_____

_____

_____

_____

_____

_____

_____

_____

_____

_____

_____

_____

_____

_____

_____

_____

_____

DATE: _____

_____

_____

_____

_____

_____

_____

_____

_____

_____

_____

_____

_____

_____

_____

_____

_____

_____

_____

_____

_____

There is a kind of magicness about going far away and then coming back all changed.

KATE DOUGLAS WIGGIN

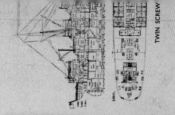

TWIN SCREW

DATE: _____

LOCATION/PORT OF CALL: _____

_____

WEATHER: _____

ACTIVITIES: _____

_____

_____

_____

_____

_____

_____

_____

_____

MEALS & DINING: _____

_____

_____

_____

_____

_____

_____

_____

DATE: _____

_____

_____

_____

_____

_____

_____

_____

_____

_____

_____

_____

_____

_____

_____

_____

_____

_____

_____

_____

_____

Time you enjoyed wasting is not wasted time.

T. S. ELIOT

DATE: _____

_____

_____

_____

_____

_____

_____

_____

_____

_____

_____

_____

_____

_____

_____

_____

_____

_____

_____

_____

_____

_____

DATE: _____

_____

_____

_____

_____

_____

_____

_____

_____

_____

_____

_____

_____

_____

_____

_____

_____

_____

_____

Light is sweet, and it pleases the eyes to see the sun.
However many years anyone may live, let them enjoy them all.
ECCLESIASTES 11:7–8 NIV

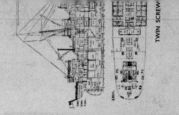

TWIN SCREW

DATE: _____

LOCATION/PORT OF CALL: _____

_____

WEATHER: _____

ACTIVITIES: _____

_____

_____

_____

_____

_____

_____

_____

MEALS & DINING: _____

_____

_____

_____

_____

_____

_____

_____

DATE: _____

_____

_____

_____

_____

_____

_____

_____

_____

_____

_____

_____

_____

_____

_____

_____

_____

_____

_____

Life is short and we never have enough time for gladdening the hearts of those who travel the way with us. O, be swift to love! Make haste to be kind.

HENRI FRÉDÉRIC AMIEL

DATE: _____

_____

_____

_____

_____

_____

_____

_____

_____

_____

_____

_____

_____

_____

_____

_____

_____

_____

_____

_____

DATE: _____

_____

_____

_____

_____

_____

_____

_____

_____

_____

_____

_____

_____

_____

_____

_____

_____

_____

_____

_____

_____

Our days are identical suitcases—all the same size—
but some people can pack more into them than others.
BITS & PIECES

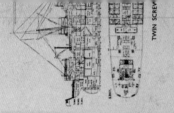

DATE: _____

LOCATION/PORT OF CALL: _____

_____

WEATHER: _____

ACTIVITIES: _____

_____

_____

_____

_____

_____

_____

_____

_____

MEALS & DINING: _____

_____

_____

_____

_____

_____

_____

_____

DATE: _____

_____

_____

_____

_____

_____

_____

_____

_____

_____

_____

_____

_____

_____

_____

_____

_____

_____

We may run, walk, stumble, drive, or fly, but let us never lose sight of the reason for the journey, or miss a chance to see a rainbow on the way.

GLORIA GAITHER

DATE: _____

_____

_____

_____

_____

_____

_____

_____

_____

_____

_____

_____

_____

_____

_____

_____

_____

_____

_____

_____

_____

DATE: _____

_____
_____
_____
_____
_____
_____
_____
_____
_____
_____
_____
_____
_____
_____
_____
_____
_____
_____
_____
_____
_____

Good company on a journey makes the way to seem the shorter.

IZAAK WALTON

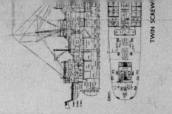

DATE: _____

LOCATION/PORT OF CALL: _____

_____

WEATHER: _____

ACTIVITIES: _____

_____

_____

_____

_____

_____

_____

_____

_____

MEALS & DINING: _____

_____

_____

_____

_____

_____

_____

_____

_____

DATE: _____

_____

_____

_____

_____

_____

_____

_____

_____

_____

_____

_____

_____

_____

_____

_____

_____

Though I have seen the oceans and mountains, though I have read
great books and seen great works of art,....there is nothing greater or more beautiful
than those people I love.

CHRISTOPHER DE VINCK

DATE: _____

_____

_____

_____

_____

_____

_____

_____

_____

_____

_____

_____

_____

_____

_____

_____

_____

_____

_____

_____

_____

DATE: _____

_____

_____

_____

_____

_____

_____

_____

_____

_____

_____

_____

_____

_____

_____

_____

_____

_____

_____

_____

_____

_____

God puts each fresh morning, each new chance of life, into our hands
as a gift to see what we will do with it.

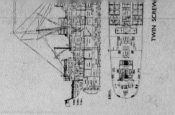

DATE: _____

LOCATION/PORT OF CALL: _____
_____

WEATHER: _____

ACTIVITIES: _____
_____
_____
_____
_____
_____
_____
_____
_____

MEALS & DINING: _____
_____
_____
_____
_____
_____
_____
_____

DATE: _____

_____

_____

_____

_____

_____

_____

_____

_____

_____

_____

_____

_____

_____

_____

_____

_____

_____

_____

_____

_____

The world is a book and those who do not travel read only one page.

AUGUSTINE OF HIPPO

DATE: _____

_____

_____

_____

_____

_____

_____

_____

_____

_____

_____

_____

_____

_____

_____

_____

_____

_____

_____

_____

DATE: _____

_____

_____

_____

_____

_____

_____

_____

_____

_____

_____

_____

_____

_____

_____

_____

_____

_____

_____

*I have wandered all my life, and I have traveled; the difference between the two
is this—we wander for distraction, but we travel for fulfillment.*

HILAIRE BELLOC

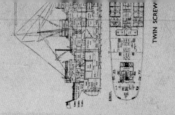

TWIN SCREW

DATE: _____

LOCATION/PORT OF CALL: _____

_____

WEATHER: _____

ACTIVITIES: _____

_____

_____

_____

_____

_____

_____

_____

MEALS & DINING: _____

_____

_____

_____

_____

_____

_____

DATE: _____

_____

_____

_____

_____

_____

_____

_____

_____

_____

_____

_____

_____

_____

_____

_____

_____

_____

I am not afraid of storms for I am learning how to sail my ship.

LOUISA MAY ALCOTT

DATE: _____

_____

_____

_____

_____

_____

_____

_____

_____

_____

_____

_____

_____

_____

_____

_____

_____

_____

_____

_____

DATE: _____

_____

_____

_____

_____

_____

_____

_____

_____

_____

_____

_____

_____

_____

_____

_____

_____

_____

_____

_____

_____

_____

Go in peace. The presence of the LORD be with you on your way.

JUDGES 18:6 NKJV

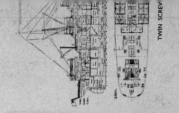

RESOURCE PAGES
HELPFUL FOREIGN LANGUAGE PHRASES

HELLO
> French: *Bonjour*
> Dutch: *Hallo*
> Spanish: *¡Hola*
> Italian: *Ciao*

THANK YOU
> French: *Merci*
> Dutch: *dank u*
> Spanish: *Gracias*
> Italian: *grazie*

GOOD-BYE
> French: *Au revoir*
> Dutch: *goede koop*
> Spanish: *adiós*
> Italian: *buon acquisto or Ciao*

WHERE CAN I GET A TAXI?
> French: *Où puis-je prendre un taxi?*
> Dutch: *Waar kan ik een taxi?*
> Spanish: *¿Dónde puedo tomar un taxi*
> Italian: *Dove posso trovare un taxi?*

PLEASE TAKE ME TO THE CRUISE SHIP TERMINUS
French: *S'il vous plaît me prendre au terminus des navires de croisière*
Dutch: *Neem me naar het cruiseschip terminus.*
Spanish: *Por favor, llévame a la terminal de cruceros*
Italian: *Vi prego di prendere al capolinea nave da crociera.*

WHERE ARE THE NEAREST PUBLIC TOILETS?
French: *Où sont les toilettes publiques les plus proches?*
Dutch: *Waar zijn de dichtstbijzijnde openbare toiletten?*
Spanish: *¿Dónde están los baños públicos más cercanos?*
Italian: *Dove sono i vicini bagni pubblici?*

WHERE IS THE NEAREST PHARMACY?
French: *Où est la pharmacie la plus proche?*
Dutch: *Waar zijn de dichtstbijzijnde apotheek?*
Spanish: *¿Dónde está la farmacia más cercana?*
Italian: *Dove sono la farmacia più vicina?*

WHERE IS THE NEAREST BANK OR ATM?
French: *Où est la banque/distributeur le plus proche?*
Dutch: *Waar zijn de dichtstbijzijnde bank of geldautomaat?*
Spanish: *¿Dónde está el banco/cajero automático más cercano?*
Italian: *Dove sono la banca più vicina o bancomat?*

INTERNATIONAL CLOTHING SIZE CONVERSION CHART

	USA	UK	FRANCE	GERMANY	ITALY	AUSTRALIA	JAPAN
X-SMALL	2	4	32	30	36	6	5
SMALL	4	6	34	32	38	8	7
SMALL	6	8	36	34	40	10	9
MEDIUM	8	10	38	36	42	12	11
MEDIUM	10	12	40	38	44	14	13
LARGE	12	14	42	40	46	16	15
LARGE	14	16	44	42	48	18	17
X-LARGE	16	18	46	44	50	20	19
1X	18	20	48	46	52	22	21
2X	20	22	50	48	54	24	23
2X	22	24	52	50	56	26	25
3X	24	26	54	52	58	28	27

FAHRENHEIT/CELSIUS CONVERSION TABLE

F	C
212	100
194	90
176	80
158	70
140	60
122	50
104	40
86	30
68	20
50	10
32	0
14	-10
-4	-20
-22	-30
-40	-40
-58	-50
-76	-60
-94	-70
-112	-80
-130	-90
-148	-100

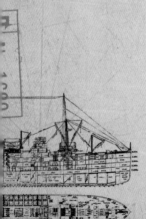

METRIC CONVERSION TABLE

LENGTH

1 inch	=	2.54 centimeters (cm)
1 foot	=	0.30 meters (m)
1 meter (m)	≅	3.28 feet
1 kilometer (km)	≅	0.62 miles
1 mile	=	1.61 kilometers (km)
1 nautical mile	=	1.85 kilometers (km)

SPEED

1 mile per hour (mph)	=	1.61 kilometers per hour
1 knot	≅	1.15 miles per hour
1 kilometer per hour	≅	0.62 miles per hour

VOLUME (LIQUID)

1 US fluid ounce	≅	29.57 milliliters (ml)
1 liter (l)	≅	33.81 US fluid ounces
1 US gallon	=	3.79 liters

VOLUME (SOLID)

1 ounce	=	28.35 grams (g)
1 pound (lb)	=	0.45 kilograms (kg)
1 kilogram (kg)	≅	35.27ounces
1 kilogram (kg)	≅	2.20 pounds (lb)

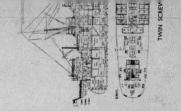

SELECT AIRLINE TOLL FREE NUMBERS

Aer Lingus 800-223-6537
Aeromexico 800-237-6639
Air Aruba 800-882-7822
Air Canada 888-247-2262
Air China 800-982-8802
Air France 800-237-2747
Air Jamaica 800-523-5585
Air Malta 800-756-2582
AirTran Airways 800-AIR-TRAN
Alaska Airlines 800-426-0333
Alitalia 800-223-5730
All Nippon Airways 800-235-9262
America West Airlines 800-235-9292
American Airlines 800-433-7300
American Trans Air 800-225-2995
Bahamas Air 800-222-4262
British Airways 800-247-9297
British Midland 800-788-0555
Cathay Pacific Airways 800-233-2742
Cayman Airways 800-441-3003
Chalk's Ocean Airways 800-4-CHALKS
China Airlines 800-227-5118
China Eastern Airlines 800-200-5118
China Southern 888-338-8988
Continental Airlines 800-525-0280
Delta Air Lines 800-221-1212
DHL WorldWide Express 800-225-5345

Dutch Caribbean Airlines 800-327-7230
El Al Israel Airlines 800-223-6700
Emirates Air 800-777-3999
EVA Airways 800-695-1188
Japan Airlines 800-525-3663
JetBlue Airways 800-538-2583
KLM 800-374-7747
Korean Air 800-438-5000
Kuwait Airways 800-458-9248
Lufthansa 800-645-3880
Mexicana 800-531-7921
Midway Airlines 800-446-4392
Pan Am 800-359-7262
Qantas Airways 800-227-4500
Ryan International Airlines 800-727-0457
SAS Scandinavian Airlines 800-221-2350
Saudia Arabian Airlines 800-472-8342
Singapore Airlines 800-742-3333
Southwest Airlines 800-435-9792
Spanair 888-545-5757
Spirit Airline 800-772-7117
SWISS 877-359-7947
TAM - Brazilian Airlines 888-235-9826
United Airlines 800-241-6522
US Airways 800-428-4322
Vasp Brazilian Airlines 866-776-3869
Virgin Atlantic 800-862-8621

CONTACTS

NAME: Kristin Garner

ADDRESS: 1824 El dorado dr.

CITY, STATE, ZIP: Acton, CA, 93510

E-MAIL ADDRESS: gotPottery@aol.Com

PHONE: 1(661) 305-6640

NOTES: My Mother

NAME: _____

ADDRESS: _____

CITY, STATE, ZIP: _____

E-MAIL ADDRESS: _____

PHONE: _____

NOTES: _____

NAME: _____

ADDRESS: _____

CITY, STATE, ZIP: _____

E-MAIL ADDRESS: _____

PHONE: _____

NOTES: _____

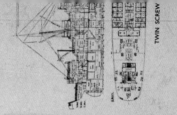

TWIN SCREW

CONTACTS

NAME: _____

ADDRESS: _____

CITY, STATE, ZIP: _____

E-MAIL ADDRESS: _____

PHONE: _____

NOTES: _____

NAME: _____

ADDRESS: _____

CITY, STATE, ZIP: _____

E-MAIL ADDRESS: _____

PHONE: _____

NOTES: _____

NAME: _____

ADDRESS: _____

CITY, STATE, ZIP: _____

E-MAIL ADDRESS: _____

PHONE: _____

NOTES: _____

CONTACTS

NAME: _____

ADDRESS: _____

CITY, STATE, ZIP: _____

E-MAIL ADDRESS: _____

PHONE: _____

NOTES: _____

NAME: _____

ADDRESS: _____

CITY, STATE, ZIP: _____

E-MAIL ADDRESS: _____

PHONE: _____

NOTES: _____

NAME: _____

ADDRESS: _____

CITY, STATE, ZIP: _____

E-MAIL ADDRESS: _____

PHONE: _____

NOTES: _____

JKL

CONTACTS

NAME: _____

ADDRESS: _____

CITY, STATE, ZIP: _____

E-MAIL ADDRESS: _____

PHONE: _____

NOTES: _____

NAME: _____

ADDRESS: _____

CITY, STATE, ZIP: _____

E-MAIL ADDRESS: _____

PHONE: _____

NOTES: _____

NAME: _____

ADDRESS: _____

CITY, STATE, ZIP: _____

E-MAIL ADDRESS: _____

PHONE: _____

NOTES: _____

CONTACTS

NAME: _____

ADDRESS: _____

CITY, STATE, ZIP: _____

E-MAIL ADDRESS: _____

PHONE: _____

NOTES: _____

NAME: _____

ADDRESS: _____

CITY, STATE, ZIP: _____

E-MAIL ADDRESS: _____

PHONE: _____

NOTES: _____

NAME: _____

ADDRESS: _____

CITY, STATE, ZIP: _____

E-MAIL ADDRESS: _____

PHONE: _____

NOTES: _____

PQR

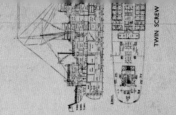

TWIN SCREW

CONTACTS

NAME: _____

ADDRESS: _____

CITY, STATE, ZIP: _____

E-MAIL ADDRESS: _____

PHONE: _____

NOTES: _____

NAME: _____

ADDRESS: _____

CITY, STATE, ZIP: _____

E-MAIL ADDRESS: _____

PHONE: _____

NOTES: _____

NAME: _____

ADDRESS: _____

CITY, STATE, ZIP: _____

E-MAIL ADDRESS: _____

PHONE: _____

NOTES: _____

CONTACTS

NAME: _____

ADDRESS: _____

CITY, STATE, ZIP: _____

E-MAIL ADDRESS: _____

PHONE: _____

NOTES: _____

NAME: _____

ADDRESS: _____

CITY, STATE, ZIP: _____

E-MAIL ADDRESS: _____

PHONE: _____

NOTES: _____

NAME: _____

ADDRESS: _____

CITY, STATE, ZIP: _____

E-MAIL ADDRESS: _____

PHONE: _____

NOTES: _____

VW

CONTACTS

NAME: _____

ADDRESS: _____

CITY, STATE, ZIP: _____

E-MAIL ADDRESS: _____

PHONE: _____

NOTES: _____

NAME: _____

ADDRESS: _____

CITY, STATE, ZIP: _____

E-MAIL ADDRESS: _____

PHONE: _____

NOTES: _____

NAME: _____

ADDRESS: _____

CITY, STATE, ZIP: _____

E-MAIL ADDRESS: _____

PHONE: _____

NOTES: _____

CONTACTS

NAME: _____

ADDRESS: _____

CITY, STATE, ZIP: _____

E-MAIL ADDRESS: _____

PHONE: _____

NOTES: _____

NAME: _____

ADDRESS: _____

CITY, STATE, ZIP: _____

E-MAIL ADDRESS: _____

PHONE: _____

NOTES: _____

NAME: _____

ADDRESS: _____

CITY, STATE, ZIP: _____

E-MAIL ADDRESS: _____

PHONE: _____

NOTES: _____

Ellie Claire® Gift & Paper Expressions
Brentwood, TN 37027
EllieClaire.com
Ellie Claire is registered trademark of Worthy Media, Inc.

Cruise Journal
© 2014 by Ellie Claire
Source material developed by Robert Koch, Quiver Global, LLC., is current at time of printing. For further reference, contact info@quiverglobal.com.
Published by Ellie Claire, an imprint of Worthy Publishing Group, a division of Worthy Media, Inc.

ISBN 978-1-60936-984-2

Compiled by Barbara Farmer
Written by Robert Koch, in partnership with Quiver Global, LLC.
www.quiverglobal.com
Cover and interior design by Gearbox | StudioGearbox.com

Printed in China

1 2 3 4 5 6 7 8 9 – 19 18 17 16 15 14

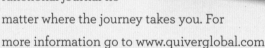